DISGUSTING ANIMAL DINNERS

Skua Seabirds Eat Vomit!

Miriam Coleman

PowerKiDS press.

New York

Published in 2014 by The Rosen Publishing Group, Inc.
29 East 21st Street, New York, NY 10010

First Edition

Editor: Joanne Randolph
Book Design: Kate Vlachos
Photo Research: Katie Stryker

Photo Credits: Cover Angelika Stern/Photodisc/Getty Images; front cover (series title) © iStockphoto.com/lishenjun; back cover graphic -Albachiaraa-/Shutterstock.com; p. 5 Glenn Bartley/All Canada Photos/Getty Images; p. 6 AndreAnita/Shutterstock.com; p. 7 Wolfgang Kruck/Shutterstock.com; p. 8 © iStockphoto.com/Giovanni Banfi; p. 9 BMJ/Shutterstock.com; p. 10 axily/Shutterstock.com; p. 11 Rick Price/Photolibrary/Getty Images; pp. 12–13 Manfred Pfefferle/Oxford Scientific/Getty Images; pp. 14, 15, 20 iStockphoto/Thinkstock; p. 17 Michael S Nolan/Age Fotostock; p. 18 Jupiterimages/Photos.com/Thinkstock; p. 19 Maksym Deliyergiyev/Shutterstock.com; p. 21 Richard Packwood/Oxford Scientific/Getty Images; p. 22 Andrey Lebedev/Shutterstock.com.

Library of Congress Cataloging-in-Publication Data

Coleman, Miriam, author.
 Skua seabirds eat vomit! / by Miriam Coleman. — First edition.
     pages cm. — (Disgusting animal dinners)
 Includes index.
 ISBN 978-1-4777-2882-6 (library) — ISBN 978-1-4777-2969-4 (pbk.) —
 ISBN 978-1-4777-3042-3 (6-pack)
 1. Skuas—Behavior—Juvenile literature. 2. Skuas—Juvenile literature. I. Title.
 QL696.C46C65 2014
 598.3'38—dc23
                                    2013022331

Manufactured in the United States of America

CPSIA Compliance Information: Batch #W14PK6: For Further Information contact Rosen Publishing, New York, New York at 1-800-237-9932

CONTENTS

Meet the Skuas

Skuas are pirates of the sky and sea. These fast and powerful birds get by in life by stealing food from other birds. Some larger skuas sometimes even kill and eat other birds.

Skuas are **predators**. They are sometimes called **kleptoparasites** because they feed off other animals by stealing from them. Their way of life may seem rude to people and annoying or dangerous to other birds. They play a role in the **ecosystem** just like any other animal in the food chain, though.

This Arctic skua, also called a parasitic jaeger, is landing on the tundra in Manitoba, Canada.

Seven Kinds of Skuas

There are seven different **species** of skuas. Four of the species make up a group called the large skuas. These are the great skua, the brown skua, the Chilean skua, and the South Polar skua. The great skua breeds on coasts and islands in the northern Atlantic Ocean. The other three large skuas all breed in the waters around Antarctica.

This is a South Polar skua. It flies along looking for food.

The great skua breeds in Iceland, Norway, the Faroe Islands, and islands around Scotland. It is seen in waters off the coast of North America, too.

The three smaller species are sometimes called jaegers. This name comes from the German word for "hunter." This group is made up of the pomarine skua, the Arctic skua, and the long-tailed skua, which is the smallest of all the skuas. These birds all breed in the Northern **Hemisphere** and head south to spend their winters somewhere warmer.

Where in the World Are Skuas?

Skuas are seabirds. They spend most of their time flying over the ocean, but they come inland to build nests. They can be found all over the world's oceans but especially in the northern parts of Europe, Asia, and North America, as well as in South America near the Antarctic.

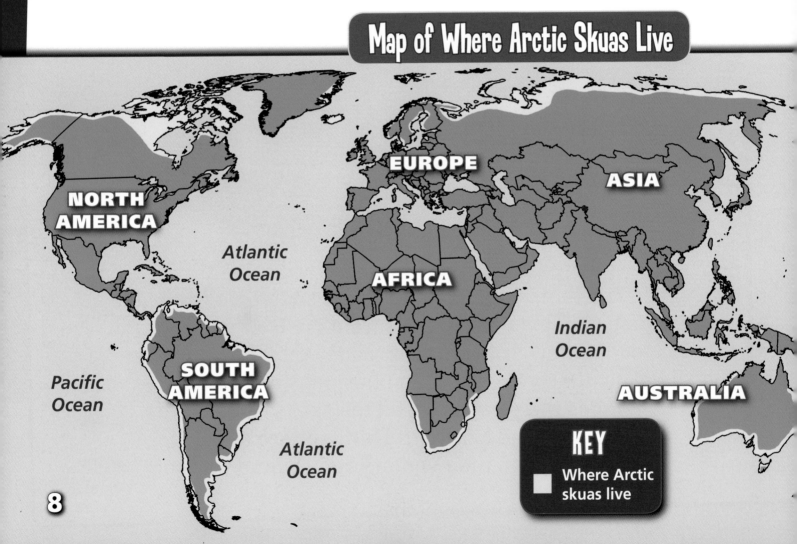

Map of Where Arctic Skuas Live

EUROPE

ASIA

NORTH AMERICA

Atlantic Ocean

AFRICA

Indian Ocean

Pacific Ocean

SOUTH AMERICA

AUSTRALIA

Atlantic Ocean

KEY

Where Arctic skuas live

Skuas spend a great deal of time in the air or resting on the seas. They fly great distances to find food and to reach breeding grounds.

Some species, such as the pomarine skua, spend their winters off the coast of West Africa. Other types of skuas, such as the great skua, live part of the year in the Arctic and then fly all the way south to the Antarctic.

Bird Bullies

Skuas have powerful, hooked claws. Their long, pointed wings make them fast fliers. The skuas' strength and speed mean that they can easily overtake other birds, such as seagulls. Skuas bully and **harass** these other birds to get their food.

Skuas are known to eat penguin eggs and chicks. This Adélie penguin is trying to tell the skua that there will be no easy meals here. The skua has its wings raised as if to say, "I'm coming in for lunch anyway."

Skuas will even attack other skuas to get their food. These two skuas are fighting over a dead penguin.

If a seagull catches a fish and is flying off somewhere safe to eat it, the skua will begin its attack. It flies in and circles around the gull, diving down at it. It forces the bird down toward the water, until the gull finally drops the fish. Then the skua quickly flies down to catch the other bird's food and eats it. Skuas will also sometimes kill and eat other birds.

DISGUSTING SKUA FACTS!

1 The South Polar skua sometimes follows ships at sea to eat the garbage that is thrown overboard.

2 Skuas have special **glands** that let them drink salt water.

3 When food is **scarce** for young skuas, an older chick may kill its younger siblings.

4 Skuas are related to gulls.

5 The Arctic skua gets almost all of its food by stealing it from other birds.

6 The great skua is the only bird that breeds in both the Arctic and the Antarctic.

7 Arctic skuas and great skuas often **compete** for the same food, and so great skuas may kill lots of Arctic skuas.

The Skua Diet

Different species of skuas feed off different foods, but most eat a lot of fish, squid, shellfish, and **carrion** they find at sea. Skuas that nest in the **tundra**, such as the pomarine skua, eat small **mammals** such as lemmings, as well as small birds, eggs, insects, and even berries.

Skuas will attack and kill other birds, especially chicks. They are also happy to eat any dead birds or other animals they find.

Brown skuas eat penguin eggs and chicks and other seabirds. They will sometimes also eat seals that are sick and weak. South Polar skuas eat a lot of fish that they steal from other seabirds.

Skuas will steal eggs from penguins' and other birds' nests and eat them.

Skuas and Vomit

Skuas don't just steal uneaten food from other birds. They also eat vomit!

We already know that skuas will bully other birds until they drop the fish from their beaks. Sometimes they go even further. Sometimes if another bird has just eaten, a skua will keep bullying and harassing the bird until it gets so frightened that it vomits up the contents of its stomach. The skua will then swoop down and eat that bird's vomit.

In the winter, vomit can make up up to 95 percent of a skua's diet. That's pretty disgusting, isn't it?

Two skuas are harassing a seagull here. If they cannot steal a fresh catch, they will help themselves to what the gull has already swallowed.

Life Cycle and Migration

Skuas may spend most of the year flying over the open ocean, but when it's time to breed, they come ashore. Many of them **migrate** long distances to reach their breeding grounds. Most skuas breed with the same partner at the same place every year.

Skuas build nests on the ground. Then, between 10 and 30 days later, skuas lay eggs. They usually lay two eggs.

These Arctic skuas, also called parasitic jaegers, migrate from the Arctic to warmer places, such as South America, South Africa, and Australia, each winter.

A mother skua sits on her nest near her two chicks.

The mother watches and defends the eggs and chicks while the father hunts for food.

The larger skua species usually breed when they are between five and eight years old. The jaegers breed when they are between one and three years old.

Baby Skuas

The two skua eggs usually hatch several days apart. Skua chicks beg for food by pecking at the parent's breast or moving up and down.

Baby skuas are covered in soft down. Jaegers sprout feathers early and grow quickly. Chicks from the larger skua species keep their down longer and put on a lot of fat to survive the Antarctic summer.

When skuas are first born, they are covered with soft, downy feathers that keep them warm in their cold habitat.

As skua chicks get older, they begin to grow regular feathers, as this one has. This young skua is spreading its wings to get its muscles ready for flying.

When young birds grow wing feathers that are large enough for flight, it is called fledging. After fledging, young skuas leave the breeding grounds. Some species remain on the open ocean until they are old enough to breed. They might not visit land at all for the first two years of their lives.

A Hard Life

Skuas are fierce and powerful birds that are good at getting what they need to survive. They are built for speed and strength.

Although their eating habits might seem disgusting to you, skuas live in a harsh world where food is not always easy to find. Flying such long distances means skuas need a lot of food to fuel them. These birds have developed the skills and stomach to take what they need.

Skuas live in some places where not many other animals can live. This skua rests on the shore in Iceland.

GLOSSARY

carrion (KAR-ee-un) Dead, rotting flesh.

compete (kum-PEET) To try to get something before another gets it.

ecosystem (EE-koh-sis-tem) A community of living things and the surroundings in which they live.

glands (GLANDZ) Organs or parts of the body that produce elements to help with bodily functions.

harass (huh-RAS) To torment someone.

hemisphere (HEH-muh-sfeer) One half of Earth or another sphere, or round object.

kleptoparasites (klep-toh-PA-ruh-syts) Animals that steal food from other animals.

mammals (MA-mulz) Warm-blooded animals that have backbones and hair, breathe air, and feed milk to their young.

migrate (MY-grayt) To move from one place to another.

predators (PREH-duh-terz) Animals that kill other animals for food.

scarce (SKERS) Small in amount, hard to find, and often wanted very much.

species (SPEE-sheez) A single kind of living thing. All people are one species.

tundra (TUN-druh) The icy land of the coldest parts of the world.

INDEX

A
Antarctica, 6
Atlantic Ocean, 6

B
bird(s), 4, 7, 10–11,
    13–14, 16, 21–22
breeding grounds,
    18, 21

C
carrion, 14
chick(s), 12, 15, 19–20

F
food chain, 4
food(s), 4, 10–14, 16,
    19–20, 22

G
glands, 12
group, 6–7

I
islands, 6

J
jaegers, 7, 19–20

K
kleptoparasites, 4

L
life, 4, 21

M
mammals, 14

N
Northern
Hemisphere, 7

P
predators, 4

S
sea, 4, 12, 14
species, 6–7, 9, 14,
    19–21

T
tundra, 14

W
water(s), 6, 11–12
winter(s), 7, 9, 16

WEBSITES

Due to the changing nature of Internet links, PowerKids Press has developed an online list of websites related to the subject of this book. This site is updated regularly. Please use this link to access the list: www.powerkidslinks.com/dad/skua/